PART 1

PART 2

BEYOND WISDOM

KEVIN ANTHONY CHEEVERS

Copyright © 2010 Kevin Anthony Cheevers

ISBN: 978-1-906027-54-4

Printed and bound in Ireland by eprint limited
www.eprint.ie

WISDOM

The knowledge and acceptance of one's ignorance is the beginning of wisdom.

Wisdom is priceless, for wise action leads to all success in life.

Wisdom frees us from unnecessary suffering and irrational fear.

Wisdom frees us from illusion and delusion.

Wisdom stills the heart and mind.

Wisdom generates virtue and thus survival for the strong willed and courageous.

Wisdom without will power and capacity for action is impotent.

The exclusive or excessive love of wisdom is unwise.

One cannot be wise without knowing it but one can be ignorant without knowing it.

Many the fools who are wise in their own eyes.

Wisdom is derivative of knowledge and understanding.

Wisdom does not violate common sense or prudence.

Everyone is wiser than you in some respect.

Inner peace and tranquility in adversity are beyond wisdom.

Everyone who seeks knowledge falls into darkness.

To attain wisdom is to emerge from darkness.

To attain wisdom is to be sage, seer and savant.

Wisdom is born of suffering and adversity.

To know what wisdom is, is to have wisdom.

I love the wisdom I seek, more than the wisdom I've gained.

Wisdom is the pursuit of truth as a guide to action and the practice of virtue as necessary to freedom and happiness.

Wisdom is rational or moral desire.

Wisdom is the application of knowledge to moral purpose.

Wisdom is to love and hate the correct things in the correct measure.

Love of virtue and hatred of vice are essential to human decency.

The Love of Truth, Justice, Virtue Beauty and Freedom is hatred of their opposites and is wisdom.

Love of Humanity conquers all tendencies to evil.

Love of self and others conquers all immorality.

The wise man is an abomination to fools as the good man is an abomination to the wicked and vice versa.

It is dangerous not to seem adequate in the eyes of the common people, good, or evil men.

It is dangerous to look too good in the eyes of the common people, good or evil men.

A man who knows the hearts of men is a very wise man and a man who knows the hearts of women is wiser still.

To love anyone or anything more than oneself is not wise for it places us in peril.

One will sacrifice only for those persons or things that one love's above oneself.

The greater one's self love, the greater one's virtue.

To know that the self in its essence and totality is beyond our comprehension, yet knowable and capable of realisation in action is probably the greatest wisdom.

Organised religion has always been an instrument of social control by the ruling classes through control of thought and emotions of the people and relations between the sexes.

The delusion that there is a supreme being or creator is the most dangerously futile belief in the world.

People of various different religions have murdered countless numbers of people throughout history in the name of their own religion. Yet history has not shown organised religion to be of any tangible value to humanity.

There are many things known that cannot be proved and many things known that are not understood.

Necessity can drive us to madness.

There are five excusable madnesses.

Love, Prophesy, Poetry, Political Fanaticism and Religious Zeal.

A little madness is essential to the attainment of personal freedom in society.

There is one essential commandment for the wise.

It is the most dangerous of all actions.

"Speak the truth when necessary in the public interest".

The philosophers kingdom is of the mind and is ideal.

The poets kingdom is of the heart and is beautiful.

The person who cannot find ideas cannot produce anything.

The person who discovers ideas produces everything.

Philosophy is war in which the victorious are those who best attain an understanding and knowledge of the Truth.

Philosophy is faith in Reason and Experience.

The aim of philosophy is the attainment of Truth; both absolute and relative, contemporary and eternal; regarding the Nature of the Universe, Humanity and Society in all their aspects and interconnections. Philosophy is faith in reason, and logic or Dialectics is the method of philosophy. The material of philosophy is human physical, sensory, emotional social and spiritual experience. The insight and understanding inherent in philosophy is derivative of the natural and social sciences and humanities.

Philosophy has evolved partly as criticism, evaluation and secularisation of religious insights and values.

Goodness only requires the absence of evil intentions and consequently the absence of evil actions.

The good do not necessarily survive.

Survival requires the capacity for evil unto evil.

Virtue is moral action and activity.

Virtue requires wisdom, willpower and courage.

The virtuous usually survive.

Some fools believe the delusion that all real success in life requires the sacrifice of one's virtue, principles and integrity.

Ultimately what "ought to be" can and will be.

To love the true ideal is wisdom.

A person who does not keep their word in little things does not keep their word in big things either.

There is one commandment for all legitimate political authority:

"Liberate the people from fear and superstition."

Socialists seek to create a better and more just society.

There is a kind of person, who knowing the power of science and information; covets knowledge and seeks to keep Humanity in ignorance; with a view to domination and exploitation of human beings in their own selfish interest. Politicians seek to bury the truth for they live by deceit, half truths lies and false promises. Politicians are "straw dogs" before the people in a democracy.

PREREQUISITES OF WISDOM

(A) 1.   To be of accurate perception.

        2.   To be of good judgement.

        3.   To be capable of sound reasoning with both facts and ideas.

(B) 1.   To be capable of control my one's emotions.

        2.   To have aesthetic and moral sensibilities.

        3.   To be strong willed.

        4.   To be strong minded enough to face reality honestly and without hypocrisy and delusion.

(C) 1.   While being sociable to maintain essential independence of thought and action.

        2.   To recognise the opposite factors of competition and co-operation in humans.

        3.   To claim no more attention than is our due.

        4.   To produce economic and social value underwriting and justifying our own existence.

        5.   To be political with regard to our class interests in society.

(D) 1.   To pursue knowledge for it's own sake and for the sake of it's application to effect change or progress.

        2.   The creation of material, social and aesthetic value.

        3.   **(a)**   Self knowledge and acceptance.

                 (b)   Understanding of human Nature devoid of romantic illusion and degenerate pessimism.

                 (c)   Self analysis and introspection or meditation.

THE MYSTIC

The Mystic is the state of inexpressible awareness of the real.

It is the cognition of truth as experiential validity.

It is the cognition of truth as is not the immediate or direct product of conscious thought activity.

It is the truth of action spontaneously correct.

It is insight attained without and separate from argument and deduction and otherwise unattainable.

It is the sense of awe and wonder at the Nature of ultimate being, the unknown.

Some truths lie beyond communication and expression.

Intuition can be either rational or irrational.

Philosophic insight originates in rational intuition.

Mystical insight is irrational intuition.

Both rational and irrational intuition have their validity.

The Primitive Reality

There is Being; objectively existent and omnipresent, composed of it's two aspects, matter and form in unity, mutually conditioning each others existence and inseparable one from the other; together substance. Nothing exists of itself alone; there is no self caused entity. All being or entity is caused to be.

Causality is infinite. The infinity of Causality is Being; now existent. To assert that an entity is or can be 'self caused' is to say that an effect can be it's own cause or that cause and effect are identical. This totally undermines the concept of causality as valid. Cause can be distinct from nor can it be identical with its effect or vice versa. There can be no science without adherence to the principle of causality and the existence of substance. The whole is Being and Nothingness in their manifestation. Nothingness is immanent in Being and vice versa.

There is logos or 'Law' immanent in the interaction of matter and form and the motion of substance. Logos is also the Nature of human thought reflecting natural reality or Being. Logos is the inherent structure of the mind derivative of objective logos or 'Law' immanent in Nature.

Logos is existent in its parallel aspects of objective and subjective, as Logos proper and Nous; the reflection of Logos as human thought process. There is individual and collective Nous reflecting objectively existent Logos inherent in the motion of substance. There is emotion, the interaction of Thought and sense Consciousness. There is the biological and physiological basis of consciousness, sensory emotional and mental. There is life, derivative of inanimate substance, a form of it's motion. Consciousness and thought are forms of motion of originally

7

inanimate substance. Thought is a form of motion of matter, which comprises the material functioning of the human brain. Consciousness sensory, emotional and mental is a material function of the living brain in the whole organism. The Unity of the Whole is contained in its Essence. The phenomena of the natural world or the Universe, whether physical chemical or biological, all have an underlying unity and coherence. The objectively existed reality has a singular indefinitely reducible essence or substance. The objectively existent infinity of matter and form, space and time has a unity and essence which will forever remain unknowable. The unity and essence of the natural world underlying the phenomenon of life and consciousness will forever remain mysterious.

NOTHING AND BEING

Nothing is the absence of everything and is therefore non- existent. Nothing is the absence of something or anything in particular; everything or all of a class. Nothing is ideal, unreal and invisible. Nothing is an impossibility. Nothing occurs of itself alone.   Nothing is uncaused and unchanging.   Nothing is INCONCEIVABLE. That which is inconceivable is impossible. Out of Nothing comes Nothing. Nothing produces or is the cause of Nothing. Nothingness is 'non- being'; it is non- existence.   Being and 'Non-being' are not mutually conditional, Being is absolute.

Reality is, always was and always will be. Because everything exists, it must always have existed, since 'nothing' comes out of 'nothing' or 'nothing produces nothing.' Being is thus uncreated and eternally existent. Being is eternal; infinite and absolute. If Being were spatially finite, 'nothing' would exist in addition to it; but since 'nothing' is nothing and materially non-existent Being is infinite and unlimited in space. Being is immanent in 'nothingness' and 'nothingness' immanent in being.

'Nothingness' or non-being is a concept of unreality; a pure ideal or negative abstraction. Being is everything such as exists now. Being is potential future and the consequent or resultant of the past. Being is indestructible and eternal. Being is the unity of becoming and 'passing away.'

THE UNIVERSE

Time is ultimate reality; all that exists, exists in time. Matter is concrete entity. Matter and Space, the displacement of matter, exists in time. Matter, Space and Time are each inconceivable separate from motion. Motion is absolute and relative. Motion is the mode of existence of matter in space and time. Matter, Space and Time are infinite as are the modes and forms of motion of matter. Space is three dimensional. Time is uni-dimensional and unidirectional. Matter is infinite in quantity, distributed in infinite space. Because matter is infinite in quantity space is infinite in extent and vice versa. Energy is a measure of the motion of matter and a mode of its existence. Matter is the direct and indirect object of the senses and the mind. Sensory effects do not exist of themselves, they are as inseparable from substance as substance is inseparable from sensory effects.

That which is perceived through the senses has objective and material existence. Matter is ultimate being of which all natural enity is composed; the bases and essence of all existence. Space is the displacement of discrete Matter. Time is the displacement of occurrence of events. Energy is the intrinsic motion of matter, and a common measure of its motion. Motion results in the displacement of matter, or its transformation from one form to another. The Universe consists of Matter in eternal motion. The Universe is infinite in space and time. The Universe is caused to be, ever was and ever will be. The Universe is caused of and by itself. The Universe is eternal SELF MOTION.

ABSOLUTE AND RELATIVE

If there is only the relative, then the relative is absolute.

The Absolute is the infinity or totality of the relative and is inherent in every aspect of the relative.

The relative contains the essence of the absolute as the absolute is the infinity of the relative.

The absolute and the relative are distinct aspects of being whose existence is mutually conditional and conditioned.

The difference between the absolute and the relative is relative.

All is either absolute; absolutely relative or relatively absolute or relative.

The absolute has unqualified and infinite existence.

The relative has qualified and infinite existence.

The absolute is ultimate Infinity.

The absolute is immutable mutability.

The relative is mutable immutability.

The immutable is the infinity and essence of the mutable.

The absolute is inconceivable without the relative and vice versa.

THE ABSOLUTE

The absolute is an object of thought and the mind alone is its reflection on the data of the senses. It is the unity, essence and whole of the universe. The absolute is the origin, genesis and totality of all that exists. It is ultimate being or substance; the unity of the material and ideal; matter and form; subjective and objective reality. It is immanent in, activates; yet transcends the material world. The absolute moves consciousness and thought as it also moves the material universe. It underlies the eternal existence of the universe and Nature. It is manifest in and through us all as life, consciousness and activity. It is manifest as the one and all. It is infinite, omnipotent, unfathomable and eternal. The attributes of the absolute are infinite. 'God' is a name for the absolute. 'God' is the 'spirit' and 'soul' of the universe; as 'soul', 'God' is the unity, essence and whole of the universe and as 'spirit', 'God' is the universal active creative power or principle immanent in the universe.

The 'soul' contains 'spirit' and 'spirit' is manifest 'soul'. The absolute is the unity of psychic and material force or being. Psychic force is ultimately material as material force is ultimately psychic. 'God' is the unity of objective and subjective being, the absolute. 'God' The absolute is ultimately reality, being or substance. The absolute is impersonal insofar as it is beyond and without us but personal insofar as it is manifest in and through us as a unique identity in a unique way. We all partake of the absolute and thus share in the Divine. The 'Love of Humanity' is inseparable from the 'Love of God' for humanity resides in 'God' and 'God' in humanity. The absolute or 'God' is an omnipotent, infinite and unfathomable power immanent in, yet transcending the material universe. 'God' is the ultimate ordering principle or cosmic law inherent in the universe.

MATERIAL AND IDEAL

The material is the basis and condition of existence of the ideal. The objective ideal is implicit in the material as form or logos. The material is the content and the ideal the form of substance. The subjective ideal is the reflection in thought or mental consciousness of the objective ideal. The ideal is inseparable from, yet as the content of thought, transcends the material. The ideal is the derivative and consequent dependent of the material. Thought is the highest known and knowable form of motion and matter. Matter is both physical concept and concrete entity. Matter is the essence and basis of objectively existing reality; matter exists outside and independent of human consciousness, it is the most important concept of science without which physics and chemistry could not exist.

There is the material, the material ideal or ideal material and the ideal. The objective ideal or logos and the subjective ideal or nous are both implicit in and form a unity within the material. There is the natural and the supernatural. The supernatural is such as remains forever inexplicable to natural science. Psychic force powers the individual and collective consciousness and subconscious of humanity; it is the power of thought process, a form of motion of matter. Psychic force causes psychic change or alterations is human mental consciousness. Psychic force can cause material change. Psychic force is synonymous with libido. Psychic force is ultimately material as material force is ultimately psychic. The spiritual is derivative of, yet transcends and acts in and upon the material. The ideal is inseparable from, yet as the content of thought, transcends the material.

CAUSAL AND ACCIDENTAL

There is the Casual and Accidental.

Accident is absolute casuality.

There is necessity and chance.

Chance is absolute necessity.

There is possibility, impossibility; probability, improbability; certainty and uncertainty.

Nothing is "uncaused", "self caused" or "cause of itself".

Causality is infinite.

The concept of a thing being 'self caused' or caused of itself makes "cause" and "effect," identical undermining the concept of Causality as objectively real and philosophically valid.

If anything were 'uncaused' everything could be 'uncaused' and the concept of Causality would likewise be undermined.

General Causality is the infinity of specific causality.

General Causality is operative through the infinity of specific causality and vice versa.

'External Causes' may be the condition of change and 'internal causes' the basis of change and visa versa.

'Every cause is the effect of a prior cause.

An effect may or may not be a subsequent cause.

Not to cause A to happen may allow B to happen as consequence.

Being is the infinity of causality existing now and eternally, both temporally and spatially.

Causality is inseparable from substance as Substance is inseparable from causality.

Substance is caused to be.

The Universe is casual of and by itself.

The Universe is matter in eternal self motion.

SUBJECTIVE AND OBJECTIVE

Absolute subjectivity is essential objectivity, though total objectivity transcends subjectivity, the Objective is independent of the subjective.

The Subjective is derivative and dependent on the Objective.

Being is:

The oneness of Mind and Matter, Matter the condition of existence of Mind; The Ideal Material or Material Ideal. Matter and Mind are distinguishable aspects not absolutely separable. Mind is mental consciousness. Thought is a form of motion of matter and carries the Ideal. Mind is the ultimate reflection of reality and the ultimate subjective reality. Human consciousness is the highest form of consciousness of Nature in Nature, known to itself alone. Creation is the comprehensive interaction of the Objective and Subjective in Nature as a specific aspect.

THOUGHT AND LOGIC

Thought is the highest form of motion of matter, a function of the living human brain. Thought is the higher concrete, containing the abstract or ideal.

Thought is a material phenomenon manifest as psychic energy. Thought is the vehicle of or carries the ideal. The thought process defines and describes the Nature, form and content of the logical and dialectical. Thought process is dialectical.

LOGIC

Logic is the form of intrinsic necessity and possibility in reality.

Logic is inseparable from the content of actuality except in the mind.

Logic is the inherent structure of the human mind reflecting the structure of objective reality.

Logic is the pattern of valid thinking which accurately reflects reality.

Logic is Reason.

Logic is the elucidation of pure concepts and fundamental ideas.

Logic is the essence of Philosophy.

Logic is the science of the laws of thought which validly reflect reality.

Mathematics is an applied logic, being a supreme synthesis of the formal, dialectical and combinatorial logic applied to number. Mathematics is the logic of the relations of number or quantity and spatial dimension and has characteristics unique to its content which it does not share with logic proper.

Formal logic always takes precedence over dialectic logic and governs it in all situations, cases and circumstances. The logic of the human mind is derivative of and a reflection of the logic of Nature. Logos is cosmic law or principle, the "logic" inherent in the Universe. Nous is human intelligence; a reflection of Logos, as thought process or mental consciousness. Dialectic is the unity of Logos and Nous. Dialectic is thought process. Dialectic is an ongoing conflict of forces, or the contradictions inherent in and manifest as the development of natural phenomena, whether stable or unstable and their reflection in thought.

Dialectics is the thought process reflecting the development of natural phenomena; the interaction of the Objective and Subjective, Matter and Mind.

Logic and Dialectics form a unity in valid human thinking. Things that are distinguishable as aspects of consciousness are separable in thought.

THE ONE

The One is the unity, essence and whole of all that exists.

The One is both objective and subjective and of myriad aspects.

The One is all, and is truth itself.

The One is the unity of the Absolute and the Relative.

The One is the infinite existent.

The One is both changing and changeless.

The One is Unlimited.

The Unity of the many is the One.

The concurrence of opposites and their unity or identity is their dissolution in the One.

The One is all that is and all that is not.

The One is certain and the One impossible.

The One is nothing and the One Being.

The One is material and the One ideal.

The One is dynamic and the One static.

The One is eternal and uncreated, the One is dark and mysterious and the One is bright and omniscient.

The One is both natural Good and Evil.

The One is neither moral Good nor Evil, but is morally neutral.

The Universe forms an identity with and is the manifestation of the One.

The One is both creative and destructive.

The One is ultimately manifest as substance and the infinite forms of its motion is infinite and eternal time-space intrinsic to which is Logos or Cosmic Law and Principle.

The One is all truth, truth is all and everything that is, has been or will be.

Truth regarding the Future is purely speculative.

Truth regarding the past is 'neutral.'

The truth of the present is material now.

THE WAY

The Way is the path of least action and resistance which effects greatest possible change in life. The Way is to consciously or unconsciously follow the Laws governing human Nature and society. The Way is to be one with what is timeless and eternal and also imperative in the Now. The Way is the recognition of natural and social necessity in our life activity. The Way is the realisation and manifestation of the true self.

In Truth and Virtue lies the way. To know the way is to be at one with one's true destiny. To be 'aimless' and 'ungrasping' is to know the way. Do not allow conscious goals to dominate your activity, and direct your course; rather be "aimless" and realise the unconscious goal or mission of your existence.

To be one with the divine is to attain the way.

The Way is neither Good nor Evil but is virtuous.

The Way is neither moral nor immoral but is indifferent.

The Way is psychic unity with the true absolute or 'God'.

Freedom from desire is essential in order to form an understanding of Humanity and Society.

The experience of desire is also necessary to an understanding of Humanity and Society.

Passivity, is essential to survival and equanimity in some circumstances.

Action is essential to survival and well being in some circumstances.

The Male is active and assertive.

The Female is passive and receptive.

The Male characteristic is courage.

The Female characteristic is endurance.

The Male is critical and aggressive.

The Female is considerable and placating.

We all have both Male and Female characteristics of personality.

GOOD AND EVIL

There is natural Good and Evil and there is moral Good and Evil. Natural Good and Evil are the biological, physiological and material condition of life and death for any species.

Deprivation of natural material, bio-social and psychological needs originating from Nature constitute natural evil. Moral Good and Evil are the conditions of life and death for any species, determined volitionally by that species itself. The Deprivation of natural material, bio-social and psychological needs of humans by the deliberate action of humans is moral evil.

Natural Evil is derivative of natural conditions. Moral Evil is a consequence of Natural Evil. Given scarce resources there is competition among humans for the satisfaction of material and bio-social as well as psychological needs. The satisfaction by humans of human needs at the expense of other humans is the origin of all moral evil. The frustration, or perversion of human needs leads humans to the satisfaction of their needs or perverted needs at the expense of other humans and is immoral evil.

There is Natural Good and Moral Good. Moral Good is derivative of Natural Good. Natural Good is the satisfaction of human needs, material, bio-social and psychological. Natural good is moral good if attained for one and all and not at the expense of some, by deliberate choice and intention and social organisation in the face of Nature. Both Natural Good and Moral Good can only be attained through deliberated human activity and organisation in the face of Nature. Natural Evil such as hunger, thirst, disease, death and the frustration of bio-social and psychological needs become moral evils if deliberately inflicted on humans by humans. The origin of all moral evil in society is a consequence of the persecution, oppression or exploitation of humans by humans in a deliberate fashion.

ANTHROPOSOPHY

It is immeasurably more important for our sanity and happiness to effect control, expression and harmony of our feelings, than it is to be pre-occupied in mental speculation as to meanings, motives and reason or objective knowledge which is inapplicable to our life situation.

HUMAN NATURE

Human needs define human Nature and determine human activity. Needs are physiological, emotional and psychological and form an integrated hierarchy. The fulfilment or frustration of any aspect of need has consequence for all other aspects. The fulfilment of needs leads to happiness and a moral life as the frustration or perversion of natural needs (which are intrinsically moral) leads to unhappiness, vice and crime.

Humans are physically, emotionally and psychologically unique and unequal. Human differences are small however by comparison with qualities held in common.

Good is the free, harmonious and all round fulfilment of human Nature, psychological, emotional and physiological. The individual is a unity of physical, sensory, emotional, mental and spiritual consciousness in confrontation with Nature and at the focus of social interaction. There are two aspects to social interaction; competition and co-operation in pursuit of individual and collective satisfaction of needs. Only that which satisfies human needs has a value for human beings.

Desire is motivation to the satisfaction of needs in humans. All natural desires are good and intrinsically moral in themselves; however the frustration, perversion or displacement and sublimation of natural needs leads to immoral and immoderate inclination. The satisfaction of individual human needs through collective organisation is the premise and raison d'etre on which all viable society is founded.

The satisfaction of individual and collective human needs, material, bio-social and psychological is the axes about which social allegiance and the presence or absence of anomie and social alienation revolve. What is good or bad for the intellectually and morally superior individual is good or bad for the common individual and vice versa. The intellectually and morally superior individual is capable of attaining greater happiness than the common individual. The intellectually and morally superior individual is capable of attaining greater joy and pleasure and the good life in benign conditions but also suffers greater pain in conditions of oppression, injustice, exploitation and persecution because of their higher moral sense and intelligence.

THE INDIVIDUAL AND THE GROUP

The individual is to themselves the experience of sensory, emotional, mental and spiritual consciousness at the focus of social interaction and relationship.

The Collective is more than the mere amalgamation of its individual members. The individual contains elements or aspects not manifest in the collective as a whole and vice versa. The group contains the interaction and social relationship of many individuals; each of whose perception differs, yet holds much in common with that of other group members.

Physical and social environment and the individuals experience of these varies considerably; though the individual in given society shares attitudes and values common to all its members. We understand the attitudes, values and experiences of others because we apprehend similar realities and because they communicate their perceptions and experiences to us.

Anomie and alienation in the individual are resultant of severe material, bio-social and psychological deprivation and are symptomatic of individual, group and class antagonism in an unjust society. Conventional Behaviour is an attempted pattern of activity aimed at social acceptance by the majority or most powerful social group or class. Unconventionalism is a statement of rejection of the values, norms and power groupings of existent society as naturally or morally wrong and unjust. Normal behaviour may be considered to be the stereotype of average behaviour in a society or the conventional manner in which most members of society "act out" on a regular basis.

Conversation, social and sexual intercourse and the experience of shared affection are all essential to mental health. The essential human values are those of the acquisition of Knowledge, Labour or Work and Sexual Love and all other values are derivative of these.

Taking action always means conflict and involvement.
Taking action always requires judgement and volition.
Only action causes change.
No action is a form of action and can cause change also.
Social being determines social consciousness which through individual and collective action alters society.
It is impossible to effect real social change without a profound philosophic and psychological insight into reality.

The agency or catalyst of social change must know and understand human nature thoroughly and the social effects of psychology. The Salvation of the individual lies entirely within themselves in interdependence with common Humanity, if at all.

THE LOVE RELATIONSHIP

Human relationships are rooted in the mutual satisfaction of material, bio-social and psychological needs. The love relationship between the opposite sexes is rooted in mutual satisfaction of biological and psychological need, given a secure economic basis. Between the sexes, the experience of desire and affection, lust and tenderness are inescapable but do not constitute spiritual love. Desire and affection, lust and tenderness; together constitute Sexual Love. Spiritual love is a derivative of Sexual Love or engenders sexual love as a consequence.

The experience of any aspect of love is necessary to the acknowledgement of its existence. True love between the sexes is the root and basis of all human morality in society.

Platonic love or agape is the true love devoid of its sexual content and is distinct from utilitarian motivated "friendship" and relationships of allegiance or solidarity if interests.

The experience of love is a greater joy and pleasure than the fantasy of love. Love relationship exists for its own sake or the satisfaction of mutual sexual and psychological needs of the partners. Love relationships exclude immorality. There is mutual responsibility of the partners for all consequences of the relationships, economic, social and psychological. The love relationship exists as necessary to the true human interests of both partners.

'Love' of anyone however to the exclusion of all others or morality, is a barbarism. The true love relationship can be founded only on a voluntary basis, that is; the exclusion of all economic, social and psychological coercion or corruption.

Love relationship of two people is based on mutual preference of each other to other available potential partners and is essentially one of spiritual, emotional and conjugal faithfulness and human loyalty. Eugenics is the concept of reproduction of the intellectually, morally and physically best possible human beings. If Eugenics is a possibility it can only occur through the natural selection by the sexes of each other on a voluntary basis and will inevitably be rooted in sexual and spiritual love, devoid of coercion corruption or utilitarian motive.

Class society has intrinsic barriers to both true love relationship between the sexes and Eugenics; for class society is rooted in the exploitation, and oppression of the people by a minority class in their own immoral and selfish interests.

ESSENTIAL ASPECTS OF HUMAN NATURE

Human beings are only partly rational in their activity. The degree of rationality of the individuals activity also varies from individual to individual. The frustration, perversion or displacement and sublimation of human needs or desires adversely affects their capacity for rationality and the operation of their conscience or moral sense.

Exploitation, injustice, oppression or persecution are the social origins of the frustration of natural human needs and desires and are the origin of all immorality in society.

THE RATIONAL HAS TWO ASPECTS

(1) The Understanding and Apprehension of natural, social and political reality and human Nature.

(2) The Emotional and Bio-Social adjustment to natural, social and political realities.

Human biological, emotional and psychological needs have an integrated and inherent logic of motivation all their own, geared to individual survival and reproduction of the human species. Natural and social environment and upbringing all affect the operation of intelligence and moral sense; genetically inherited by the individual from their parents.

Deprivation of Psychological, bio-social and material needs all adversely affect the operation of innate intelligence and moral sense in the individual and can be of disastrous social consequence if replicated on a significant scale.

The 'rational' individual is one who has best employed their intelligence through moral sense, in the satisfaction of psychological, bio-social and material needs. The rational is a unity and harmony of the Mental, Emotional and Bio-Social in the individual and society at large. Individuals and societies both can become pathological and inimical to their own survival due to mal adjustment to natural and historical developments and constraints resulting and resultant in mass psychological, bio-social or material deprivation and social psychosis. Crises in society inevitably results in social violence consequent of extreme deprivation of human needs on a significant scale. Genocide is the worst barbarism.

THE HUMAN EMOTIONS ARE

1. Love and Hate
2. Fear and Anger
3. Vanity and Humility
4. Joy and Sorrow
5. Envy and Jealousy

The first four operate as a unity or conflict of opposites. Thus Love and Hate operate as opposite emotions in the individual. They can augment or annihilate each other as with Fear and Anger; Vanity and Humility; Joy and Sorrow; one or other of the opposite poles can become dominant or generalised. Thus hatred of injustice consolidates and augments love of justice and there is also mutual balance of the force of these opposite emotions.

Love or hatred of a person or thing however may become generalised and dominant if there is no balance and may become a primary attitude or motivation. One dominantly motivated by love is constructive and creative. One dominantly motivated by hatred is destructive and vicious. One dominated by fear may act in a cowardly fashion. One dominated by anger may act in a rash or arrogant or aggressive manner. One dominated by vanity may be a boaster and a braggart; while one dominated by humility may be self effacing to the point of loss of confidence and dignity or poise.

Envy motivates us to competition (both moral and immoral). Jealousy results from the appreciated denial by others of the satisfaction of needs we acknowledge all have a right to, or results from the deprivation of individual needs and desires by the selfish and immoral actions and advantages of others. Envy and jealousy both are anti-social and malignant emotions; though often justified and necessary to positive or progressive social change of a destructive nature.

BIOLOGICAL NEEDS

The frustration, perversion, displacement or sublimation of sexual and reproductive needs results in serious irrationality of behaviour and can result even in psychotic breakdown. If of mass social significance it can be of the nature of a severe political, social and economic crisis of society, culminating in either political reaction or revolution.

The general satisfaction of Biological needs in society is symptomatic of the satisfaction of material, social and psychological needs and is essential to a politically healthy society.

The general satisfaction of material, bio-social and psychological needs in society is essential to the possibility of just social and political order and economic reproduction.

The 'bio-social' alienation of classes or groups or religious sects in society leads to violence and terror in society of an often intractable nature.

Crime and vice in society are concommitants of a significant scale of deprivation of human needs as a consequence of generalised anomie and alienation.

PAIN AND PLEASURE

Pleasure is generally good and wholesome. Pain is generally evil and unwholesome. Pleasure such as negates pleasure is bad. Pain such as negates pain is good. The absence of either pain or pleasure is neither good nor bad. Anything solely the cause of pleasure only is good. Anything solely the cause of pain only is bad.

Anything solely the cause of both pain and pleasure is neither good nor bad or a mixture of good and bad. There is no such thing as pleasurable excess, all excess leads ultimately to pain or is painful in itself. Pleasure and pain may be physical, emotional, mental or spiritual. Spiritual pleasure is joy. Spiritual pain is sorrow. Pleasure and pain may differ in degree and quality. The pleasure of each sense is qualitatively different from the pleasure of each other sense. The pleasure of the senses combined is qualitatively different from the pleasure of any single sense. Mental and spiritual pleasure are qualitatively different from the pleasures of the senses. Emotional pleasure or pain is the link between sensual mental and spiritual pleasure or pain. Happiness is the fulfilment or satisfaction of natural needs. Natural desire is motivation to the satisfaction of natural needs. There is desire for pleasure and enjoyment. There is desire for the end and goal of all desire. Attainment of the end and goal of all desire is the cessation of desire. There is desire for the cessation of desire. There is desire for the cessation of suffering. The true 'hearts desire' is sexual love union or love-longing. The ultimate movement of desire is for psychic union with the true Absolute, 'God' or the Spirit and Soul of the Universe. All natural desire is moral; only the frustration or perversion of natural desire leads to immorality and unhappiness or suffering. Sexual orgasm is physical union combining sensual, emotional and mental sympathy with the opposite sex. Sexual orgasm is the closest possible union of two people of the opposite sex, which union is sensual, emotional and spiritual.

ASPECTS OF THE PERSON

The nature of the human person may be encompassed four, spirituality, mentality, emotion and sensuality. In the healthy person these aspects operate as an integrated harmony of personality. These aspects comprise a unity of psyche, sense and soma. These three aspects correspond with the three aspects of love between the sexes.

Love of mind or psyche.

Love of heart or love longing.

Love of body or sensual attraction.

CONDITIONING

1. Only desires, reflexes, drives or feelings can be conditioned.

1.1. Only I and I alone can know my own mind and my own psychological state.

1.2. The ego, that which out of the depths of mind unconscious of itself utters "I" the "I" that thinks, feels and experiences, the Will; this existential "I" in its utterance both proves and verifies "ego" and "self,": logically and existentially respectively.

1.3. The 'I' is inviolable in life. The origin of my thought is unconditioned; though my sensory consciousness may or can be. The great are great because they suffer and endure for the universal cause.

1.4. I think therefore I am.
I see therefore I am.
I feel therefore I am.
I am, whether I see, feel or think or not.
I am who I am.
I who think and know 'I' prove and verify my own existence.
I am at the centre of my sensations, thought, emotional and sensual experience, my existential 'self'.
'I' am my greatest possession.

PSYCHOLOGICAL SELF RULE

1.1 The human individual is both a social and sexual animal.

1.2 The higher human Nature may be accurately described as a unity of the philosophical and psychological.

1.3 The objective world or universe of which we generally remain incognizant, underlines all the actualities and possibilities such as dialectic interaction brings into being or causes to be.

1.4 The objective world, or Universe is reflected in the totality of human consciousness; mental, emotional and sensory.

1.5 We remain aware of the rudimentary form and aspects of the capacity of retention, recognition and recollection. We also experience and can analyse the significance of dreams and are aware of the process of mental incubation, which precedes subsequent intuitive insights.

1.6 In the face of Nature and society we grow either in peace and harmony or in the transcendence and overcoming of pain and suffering.

1.7 The individual contains four irrefutable aspects to their consciousness.

(1) The 'Id' or instinctual wisdom based on the avoidance of pain and the pleasurable gratification of the senses and basic drives. This instinct is genetically transmitted and culturally reinforced or effaced.

(2)   The 'Super Ego' or innate conscience or moral sense genetically transmitted and culturally and psychically shaped.

(3)   The 'Ego' that which thinks and it's internal reflection of itself; such as is exemplified when we think "I" and are aware of ourselves thinking "I" and the self image respectively.

(4)   'Libido' is life-force and inseparable from sexual potency and physical vigour. It powers the thought process and is the source of all energy expended psychically and sexually. The Id seeks to avoid pain and pursue pleasure. The libido powers both psychic and sexual human operation. The super ego strives to allow the Id have its way insofar as it does not violate the ethical code which is written in our genes and culturally shaped. The ego is the conscious or subconscious aspect of mind which integrates super ego and Id and leaves Id free within the limits to which ego has rationalised the super ego and Id. Any aspect of consciousness; super ego, ego, Id or Libido may in certain life situations be the dominant aspect of consciousness or the subconscious and determine behaviour.

1.8   There are two aspects of brain activity which penetrate our mental consciousness.

They are:
(a)   Conscious mind.
(b)   Subconscious or unconscious mind.

1.9   Conscious mind is the dominance of the ego.

2.0   Subconscious or unconscious mind generates spontaneously the basis of stored but unrecalled memories. What is suitable for application in the immediate contemporary reality becomes conscious and is operated on.

2.1   The conscious mind is not necessarily dominant with regard to the subconscious mind, yet it is certainly so during thought activity which would fall within the context of logic proper in its more general and particular aspects.

2.2   If there are unresolved contradictions exciting in our subconscious, then there is conflict between super ego and Id which has not been resolved, the individual being a moral or ethical 'schizophrenic'.

2.3   The conscious mind may direct and control the subconscious by auto-suggestion or by the exclusion of externally generated suggestion or conditioning.

2.4   Resolutions of thought and feeling and their interaction have inevitably positive consequences for the individual, their character structure, absence of guilt and genital confidence.

2.5   When through the exercise of ego we eliminate such phantasms or wrong notions as have permeated our subconscious; becoming essentially "ego-centric, "we generate an effacement of subconscious conflict.

2.6   When integrated through the ego, we have Id and super-ego convergent on moral issues; the power of the Libido is utilised for positive good and the strengthening of mind, while the ego will subsequently and consequently operate at its best.

2.7 We are now left with a residue which is no more or less than the natural integration and conflict-free harmonious unity of self, with good society and ultimately with the wondrous awesomeness and omnipotence of the Universe.

2.8 Dominance over and control of immediate situational reality is a pre-condition for general success in all endeavour.

2.9 Self imposed birth control distinguishes Humanity from the animals more than any other single factor.

3.0 Fearlessness is the absence of ignorance, based on objective knowledge and subjective insight.

3.1 The harmonious integration of Super Ego and Id through egoistic rationalism results in a harmonious correspondence of conscious and subconscious mind and unity of psyche sense and soma.

3.2 The division of mind into the aspects of conscience, instinct and rationality innate and common to us all, as well as asserting the existence of the subconscious as underlying the conscious, are intuitively brilliant and psychologically irrefutable perceptions of Freud. That psychological harmony of the individual is inextricably connected with the balanced interactor of these aspects of the psyche; few of introspective experience or acute observation of the behaviour of others will doubt. Consciousness consists of thought, emotion, sensation and will.

Subconscious mind is a gathering of knowledge and wisdom attained by the conscious mind and stored for active use. The subconscious mind has a teleology, direction and goal of its own, distinct from conscious will; which acts in either harmony or conflict with conscious will. The id is subconscious instinct gathered over generations and genetically transmitted; related to physiological, biological and psychological needs and their satisfaction.

ONESELF

I am first and foremost, totally myself.

If I do not possess myself, I possess nothing and am at the mercy of all.

I am no more and no less than myself, the totality of what I think, feel, experience and do.

I am the existential "I," a soul - and at the centre of that soul is a will.

I am not a name, number, category, occupation, title, class member or a distinction as such.

I am not a collection of wealth or poverty.

I am a unique person in all respects.

"I" am my greatest possession.

I am a the centre of my being a will and should will:

(a) The satisfaction of all my natural needs and desires.

(b) The attainment of self-realisation and manifestation.

(c) All-round psychological, bio-social and physical development.

I have the will to:

1. Survival
2. Sex and Reproduction
3. Love and Friendship
4. Power and Freedom
5. Truth and Justice
6. Fame and Fortune

Will power requires:

A. Self-respect
B. A self-ideal
C. A general life goal
D. Organised and habitual creative and routine activity or work

Will power is the actualisation of our heart's desires and intentions.

Decide for the good;

Will the good;

Choose the good;

Act for the good - of oneself and all.

Wealth, power and fame are not to be sought for their own sakes and are joyless if obtained at the expense of health and happiness.

The meaning of life is to be found in the attainment of personal happiness.

Act, do and be only what is necessary or what you will.

I know myself existentially in the now; yet I will never fully understand myself.

The person is not merely what they are in relation to other people; they are what they are essentially to themselves.

I cannot love others unless I love myself and vice versa.

I cannot respect myself unless I respect others and vice versa.

We love ourselves only if we love the common humanity of which we are a part.

We all have to make an act of faith in ourselves and humanity.

Any philosophy which debases the value of the individual person is opposed to the common interest of humanity ultimately.

What is important about the person is their intentions and what they are capable of doing.

Wisdom, virtue and love of humanity are highly desirable attainments.

Soul is the essence of the individual human.

Soul is also the common humanity.

Soul is the centre of consciousness and also the subconscious.

Ego, the rational and existential identity of the individual, is soul.

The ego thinks, wills and feels emotions and sensations.

It is self-aware and self-interested.

Will directs our activities to the satisfaction of natural desires, needs and life goals. Goals are conscious and subconscious aims in life. Desire is spontaneous feeling directing our activity to the satisfaction of natural needs.

The will integrates the personality and determines the extent, kind and success of our life activity.

RATIONAL FEARS

Fear is a great cause of suffering.

Rational fears are:
(1) Fear of violence
(2) Fear of physical illness
(3) Fear of destitution
(4) Fear of vice and crime
(5) Fear of corruption and exploitation
(6) Fear of deception
(7) Fear of rejection and isolation
(8) Fear of persecution and oppression or exploitation and marginalisation

PROBLEMS OF LIFE

Problems facing the individual in the pursuit of health and happiness are:

(1) The Material Problem

The problem of acquiring life's material economic necessities.

(2) The Social Problem

The problem of social classes, exploitation, oppression, persecution and injustice. We must overcome, eliminate or endure social injustice where immediate change is impossible. Ultimately, collective social and political action, combined with science and economy, eradicates these problems where they bear on the material problem.

(3) The Problem of Understanding

There is:

(a) Objective Reality, or the world external to ourselves, of which we are a part.

(b) Subjective Reality, or the world of our sensations, emotions and thought.

(c) The Relationship of the Subjective to the Objective and vice versa.

(d) The relationship of individual psyches.

(e) The relationship of individual subjective reality and collective subjective reality.

It is the interaction of (d) and (e) which generates art and self-knowledge and (c) which generates science. The problem is to know and understand Nature, society and humanity.

Attainment of knowledge requires the following:

(A) Factual knowledge

(i) Discovering and comprehension of facts

(ii) The weighing and comparison of facts.

(iii) Predicting hitherto unobserved facts.

(iv) Perceiving the consistency and interrelation of facts.

(B) Explanation

The relation and comparison of ideas and concepts representing or reflecting reality.

(i) Theoretical exposition

(ii) Logical coherence, consistency and correspondence

(iii) 'Clarity' and 'Simplicity'.

(4) The Problems of Emotion

The problems of emotion is that of achieving stable, balanced and appropriate experience of and the controlled expression of emotion to a great extent what we 'perceive' and think determines how and what we feel.

The subconscious processes behind our dispositions of attitude and thought are instrumental in evocation of emotional response.

(5) The Problem of Volition

(A) Will is the process of instigation, direction maintenance and organisation of effort and activity to the accomplishment of goals. The problem of volition is in part the problem of motivation. The individual must want to attain particular goals which must be related to the satisfaction of psychological, emotional, bio-social and physiological needs.

(B) Will is the facility of making rational decisions and adhering to them.

(C) Will is the ability to do such as is necessary, whether to our inclination or not.

(D) Will is the able assertion of self-interest in line with objective necessity and possibility.

(E) Will is the ability to submit oneself to rational discipline of a self or externally imposed kind of an imperative nature.

(F) Will is the ultimate assertion of self. The will activates the person to the satisfaction of natural needs and desires.

(6) The Problem of Action

Action is thought or emotion.

Action is the expression of thought or emotion.

Action is speech or gesture.

Action is physical movement or biological function.

Action can combine any or all of the foregoing.

Action involves risk and uncertainty.

Action means involvement and conflict.

Action requires judgement and volition.

Action often requires courage.

Clearly action changes reality.

Inaction is a form of action and has its own consequences.

Be active in the NOW!

7. The Sexual Problem

The sexual problem stated, is the Natural Ongoing requirement of the human person for sexual copulation and orgasm if neurosis and irrational thinking or behaviour are to be avoided.

The frustration or perversion of natural sexual needs, leads to considerable suffering of a psychosomatic character. The sexuality of a person cannot be separated from either their mentality or personality and if we are not neurotic no member of the opposite sex can be seen merely as a 'sex object.' They are all persons of particular and unique mentality and personality. Attraction of mentality, personality and sexuality are all essential to satisfying love relationships between the sexes.

The bio-social alienation of classes, religious sects and political groupings in society militates against natural selection by the sexes of each other on the basis of spiritual and sexual love. Economic and social factors currently existing in class society adversely affect egalitarian love and natural eugenics.

The Threefold Origin of Suffering:

1. Suffering originates either from within ourselves or is derivative of the natural world or society.

2. Suffering originating from within ourselves arises from ignorance of our own true Nature and our hearts desires and ignorance of human Nature in general.

3. Suffering originating from within can also arise from an underlying disunity of thought, a failure to develop a unitary world view through rational holistic association and logic. A 'compartmental' mind results.

4. An underlying disunity of thought is a failure of conscious reasoning or conflict between conscious and subconscious mind or both.

5. Suffering arising from within ourselves may have the aspect of fear of being honest with ourselves about our true hearts desires and how they interact with social reality. We may be "hiding from ourselves."

6. Suffering originating in the physical world and society is derivative of constraints that frustrate or pervert our natural needs and desires.

7. Natural needs are physical, biological, emotional psychological and social. Human needs form an integrated hierarchy, the frustration of any aspect of need affects all others and alters human motivation and personality.

The ego is a unity of sensory and mental consciousness, comprising will, intellect, emotion and sensation at the focus of social interaction in confrontation with Nature.

8. Happiness is the satisfaction of natural needs and desires; which are generally of a moral nature.

9. Unhappiness is the frustration or perversion of natural needs and desires and usually leads to immoral Behaviour.

10. Moral Behaviour implies happiness whereas immoral Behaviour is synonymous with unhappiness.

11. True happiness is a moral life.

12. In virtue lies happiness.

13. Virtue requires wisdom and willpower.

14. Injustice, oppression, exploitation and persecution are the ultimate social causes of suffering.

15. Violence, disease and material deprivation are the natural origins of suffering.

16. All three causes of unhappiness; personal social and natural augment and consolidate each other.

The Causes of Suffering Elaborated:

1. Unfilled love-longing or loneliness.

2. The frustration or perversion of natural desires.

3. Obsessional or immoral desire.

4. Fear based on ignorance or belief.

5. Craving for the unattainable.

6. Craving for illusory good in ignorance of the true good.

7. Ignorance of necessity and possibility.

8. Selfishness and greed.

9. Vanity.

10. Unjustified discontent.

11. An underlying disunity of conscious thought.

12. Injustice, persecution, oppression and exploitation.

13. Violence, disease and material deprivation.

14. Psychological, Social or Material insecurity.

Happiness:

Happiness is the satisfaction of natural needs and desires; psychological, bio-social and material.

Happiness is the self realisation, manifestation and fulfilment of the persons innate potentiality; spiritual, intellectual, emotional and bio-social and is the ultimate good.

Happiness is joy and pleasure.

Unhappiness is suffering and pain.

Unhappiness results from persecution, oppression, exploitation and injustice.

Unhappiness results from the frustration or perversion of natural needs which leads to immorality, vice and crime.

Happiness Generally Results From:

1. Sexual Love
2. Platonic Love or friendship
3. Music, Song and Dance
4. All Creative, productive and useful work
5. Material, social and psychological security
6. Freedom and Power
7. Justice
8. Virtue
9. The absence of suffering

Happiness is the end and goal of natural desire.

Desire motivates humans to the satisfaction of natural needs.

There is desire for the satisfaction of natural needs.

There is desire for pleasure and enjoyment.

There is desire for the end and goal of all desire.

Attainment of the end and goal of all desire or the satisfaction of natural needs is the cessation of desire.

The True 'hearts desire' is sexual love union or love-longing.

Desire ultimately moves to the desire for psychic union with the true absolute or 'God', Spirit and soul of the Universe.

There is desire for the cessation of suffering.

The Nine Great Happinesses:

1. Psychic union with the true absolute or 'God'; Spirit and Soul of the Universe.
   'The Love of God'

2. Sexual Love Union
   Psychological, emotional and physical.
   "Love of the Sexes"

3. Psychic and Social Integration with Good Society or the absence of alienation or anomie.
   'The Love of Humanity'

4. Creative Art and Literature

5. Performing Arts

6. Service To Humanity
   "The Cause of the People"

7. Political Power and Freedom

8. Investigative Science and Invention

9. Material, social and psychological security.

Moral Absolutes:

It is wrong to take life except as necessary to preserve our own or another or as a lesser evil.

Sexual prostitution and incest are immoral and natural evils both.

The persecution, oppression or exploitation of others is always wrong.

It is wrong to constrain the individual in any way except in their own interest or the common good.

There are two fundamental processes of mind:

1. That of effecting Understanding of Reality.
2. That of effecting Emotional Adjustment to Reality.

   The rational is a unity or synthesis of these two processes which determines our capacity for action and our degree of initiative and success.

THE TWELVE HINDRANCES

VANITY, SELFISHNESS, GREED, DISTRACTION, WORRY, DOUBT, IGNORANCE, STUPIDITY, LAZINESS, ILLWILL, FEAR AND LUST.

THE TENFOLD DISCIPLINE

1. Right Concentration

2. Right Vision

3. Right Mindfulness

4. Right Aspiration

5. Right Occupation

6. Right Association

7. Right Purpose

8. Right Action

9. Right Speech

10. Right Effort

1. Right Concentration

Combines four stages of meditation:

(a) Thought and Deliberation

(b) Inner Serenity resulting from Thought and Deliberation

(c) Well being, devoid of joy or sorrow, Thought and Deliberation and suffering

(d) Equanimity, which is neither Well being nor Suffering, Joy or Sorrow, Elation or Dejection, Thought or Deliberation

2. Right Vision

To perceive the causes and origins of joy and sorrow, well being and suffering and their cessation.

3. Right Mindfulness

The observation of our sensations, emotions and thought so as to be cognisant of the origin and cessation of suffering and dejection and guard against the perversion of natural desire through deprivation or excess.

4. Right Aspiration

To aspire to attain Truth, Justice, Freedom and Beauty in living.
To aspire to wisdom, virtue, happiness and the true good.

5. Right Occupation

To earn one's livelihood honestly and in a capacity suited to our talents and abilities.

6. Right Association

To associate only with morally decent individuals and avoid the company of criminals and degenerates.

7. Right Purpose

To aim to do good and oppose evil when possible or necessary. To renounce apparent good and wrong ambition for true good and right ambition.

8. Right Action

Not to take life, except to preserve our own or another's or as the lesser evil. Not to rob or steal. To reject rape, incest and prostitution.

9. Right Speech

To be generally truthful and avoid vain dispute and malicious gossip.

10. Right Effort

To exert oneself suitably so as not to fall into degenerate pessimism and unwholesome states of mind.

HUMAN VIRTUES

1. Truthfulness

Integrity, honesty and sincerity in speech and action.

2. Temperance

Moderation of appetites and desires.

3. Liberality

Generosity within one's means.

4. Justice

Fairness to everyone in all one's dealings.

5. Sociability

Friendliness towards all except one's enemies and criminals or degenerates.

6. Courage

Bravery, moral, social and physical, in the face of intimidation or injustice, oppression, exploitation or persecution.

7. Pride

Proper self-esteem precluding vanity and humility.

8. Magnanimity

Appropriate self-assessment, being cognisant of the highest human standards of relevance.

9. Right Ambition

To seek to advance by honest means to the satisfaction of material, social and psychological needs and desires.

10. Modesty

Neither shyness, shame nor shamelessness. Neither boastfulness nor exaggeration.

11. Righteousness

To be right living and denounce wrong conduct in all things. To be neither envious nor malicious.

12. Hedonism

The pursuit of ultimately pleasurable and joyful experience and the avoidance of pain and suffering when possible.

13. Fortitude

To be able to endure pain and suffering for the ultimate gain of good.

14. Wittiness

Neither buffoonery nor boorishness in conversation but good humour and sharpness of mentality.

15. Patience

Neither irascibility nor lack of spirit. Being slow to anger but capable of fight.

16. Magnificence

Neither vulgarity nor pettiness.

17. Conscientiousness

Neither carelessness nor irresponsibility.

ESSENTIAL FREEDOMS

1. Freedom from oppression, exploitation, injustice and persecution.

2. Freedom from material, social and cultural poverty or depravation.

3. Freedom of thought, speech, communication and publication.

4. Freedom of moral or non-criminal association.

5. Freedom to do that which is the interest of one and all and not to do that which is not the interest of one and all.

6. Freedom of physical movement or travel.

7. Freedom of religion or no religion and atheism.

8. Freedom of political opinion and allegiance.

9. Freedom to do what's right and not to do what's wrong for oneself or others.

10. Freedom from compulsion with regard to action which is harmless to oneself or others.

11. **Personal Freedoms**

   Freedom to Love

   Freedom to study and investigate

   Freedom to create

   Freedom to travel and experience

   Freedom to grow and develop

   Freedom of leisure

Omnipotent and infinite unfathomable power, eminent in, yet transcending the natural world, underlying and sustaining all existence and manifest in and through us all as life consciousness and activity:

May I attain unity with the One and All.

May I find psychic unity with "God," Spirit and Soul of the Universe.

May my will attain to an identity with the Divine and Universal Will and the general Will of Humanity.

May I attain the Way, the Truth and the Life.

Grant me freedom, justice, equity and humanity.

Grant me a life free of suffering, dejection and despair; I seek only the true good.

Almighty and Eternal God, Spirit and Soul of the Universe, may I be an instrument of the Divine and Universal Will in harmony with the General Will of Humanity.

May I be free from fear and anxiety, despair and loneliness.

INTERCAUSAL ASPECTS OF PSYCHIC AND SOCIAL BEING

1. There is the Absolute comprising the unity, essence and whole of both objective and subjective reality - the unity of the material and ideal.

    The Absolute is manifest in and through everyone as life and consciousness and activity, an integrator of psyche, sense and soma and rooted in the individual and collective subconscious.

2. The material is the indefinitely reducible substratum of reality, the ideal, its form. They together constitute substance.

3. Thought is a form of motion of matter, the content of which is ideal.

4. When thinking "I am," the thought process is a material form of motion of matter; the content "I am" is, however, ideal, despite its existential veracity. Thus, my existence, both sensuous and mental, is material, though mental consciousness carries the ideal.

5. Individual consciousness, an integration of sensory, emotional and mental consciousness, is a unified whole.

6. Logos is the objective form of existence of the modes and motion of matter.

7. Nous in the subjective reflection of logos as individual and collective thought process.

8. Logos and nous are congruent as dialectic and comprise a unity of the material and ideal which is thought or mental consciousness, manifest through the life activity and being of individual and collective humanity.

9. Individual being or the person is material, containing in consciousness a unity of sensuality and thought, reflecting objective reality of which it is a manifestation.

10. Collective being or humanity comprises the totality of all existent persons, their individual and collective consciousness, mental, emotional and sensory and their collective subconscious.

11. Collective consciousness and sub-consciousness, through communication at both these levels, are common to all individual humanity in various degrees, related to individual awareness and through spontaneous thought and activity.

12. There is sensory perception and extra-sensory or mental perception, both being integrated and whole images of objective physical and psychic reality.

13. There is telepathy or the transfer of thought and perceptions between individuals which transcends oral and written communication.

14. Collective consciousness and sub-consciousness are something shared more or less by all humanity.

15. Humanity as a whole is a slave to the necessity of biological and economic reproduction as necessary for the survival of the species.

16. Social being determines human social consciousness, which in turn affects and alters social being.

17. Human consciousness as knowledge shared and implemented in bio-social and economic activity changes natural and social reality and humanity itself in the process.

18. Shared human consciousness is a collective material force for the transformation of the world, whether good or evil.

19. Truth shared in social consciousness is a collective material force for progress, whereas falsehood and delusion are material forces generating regression.

20. Collective or shared consciousness and sub-consciousness are the psychological forces of all mass movements.

21. The leadership of mass movements shares the psychological consciousness and sub-consciousness and the bio-social character of their mass following.

22. Character structure in the individual is a unity of sensory, emotional, mental and bio-physiological consciousness and awareness.

23. Humanity is an incarnate manifestation of bio-social, economic and material force with the Absolute as its apex.

24. Economic and bio-social reproduction are inextricably connected and determined by the level of transcendence of humanity over Nature.

25. The material transcendence of humanity over Nature depends on the level of sophistication of political, natural, social and economic sciences and their application.

26. The level of sophistication of technology and economic science determines the degree or scale of bio-social reproduction of humanity.

27. The collective morality of humanity is instrumental in determining the degree and quality of civilised living possible, and at the same time human morality cannot generally rise above the level of material transcendence of the individual over Nature; collectively in society.

28. Both subjective or psychic and material economic conditions determine social and political evolution and revolution.

29. All revolutions are preceded by revolutions in thought and collective consciousness of the people as well as changes in mass morality and sexual mores.

30. All revolutions are consequent of fundamental change in the collective consciousness and material conditions of life of the people.

31. All revolutions are a result of major changes in the bio-social activities and organisation of the masses.

32. The collective morality of the masses does not rise generally above economic and material survival necessities in a crisis.

33. The degree of violence and moral regression inherent in revolutionary change of a violent character is determined by the degree of change in objective, material, economic and social conditions and respective collective consciousness.

A CONCEPTION OF HUMANITY

Human needs define human Nature and determine human activity. Humanity exists materially, socially, culturally and spiritually in itself and must come to exist for itself in all aspects.

Human needs are psychological, social and biological. When human needs go unsatisfied, human beings are discontented and pursue substitute artificial wants to an insatiable degree. Where human needs are fulfilled or satisfied, selfishness and greed die. When human needs are frustrated or perverted, human beings suffer and are unhappy and pursue the satisfaction of their needs or perverted needs at the expense of their own and other people's well being, and humanity as a whole is poorer.

Happiness is the satisfaction and fulfilment of natural human needs and desires, as unhappiness results from their frustration or perversion.

PSYCHOLOGICAL NEEDS

Psychological needs consist of a range of satisfactions imperative to happiness and the non-neurotic functioning of the individual in society.

Psychological needs are the apex of human need and comprise the psychic or spiritual and the mental.

Spiritual needs are the unconscious needs within humans for harmony within themselves and between themselves and others, Nature and society.

72

Psychic or spiritual needs constitute the searching of the individual for ultimate meaning in life, a search for "God, " the way, the truth and the life. A search for the nature and end of all existence. A philosophical orientation in natural and social reality.

Mental need is the innate compulsion of the human person to know, understand, express and control reality in their own interest and in their own way.

The individual need to control one's own level and quality of material and social existence is the compulsion on which all material progress rests.

The need to know, express and understand necessary for this is the raison d'etre of all human culture.

Psychological needs require the possibility of full development of a person's mental abilities and the all-round development of character and personality.

A person whose intellectual growth has been stunted by adverse social circumstances necessarily suffers.

Psychological needs require the possibility of growth and freedom if they are to be fulfilled.

Restriction of social or material circumstances or political oppression, persecution or economic exploitation all adversely affect the fulfilment of innate mental potential and consequent development of character and personality.

SOCIAL NEEDS

Once we go beyond the individual to the number two or more, we have society and the satisfaction of needs, properly called social. They are social in that they can only find satisfaction in and through human company.

First and foremost is the innate compulsion to love and be loved. A person unloved or un-loving is only a human tragedy, and not to be loved or not to love is incapacitating.

By love, I mean both affection and sexual desire. One naturally, at least originally, has an affection for all decent people and desire for biological fulfilment through the opposite sex. If the need for affection and sexual gratification is frustrated or perverted, we have intense individual suffering, anomie and alienation in society and consequent social evil.

We only love the beautiful and hate only the ugly. Beauty is the quality of a thing or person whereby they are loved, and ugliness is the quality of a thing or person whereby they are hated.

Consequently, as we all want to be loved, we all wish to be beautiful, and self-love is rooted in the perception of one's own beauty, as love of others resides in the perception of their beauty by us. The perception of beauty is subjective, but beauty itself is an objective quality.

Beauty is of form, colour, mode, substance, sensation and utility in all their objective connotations. Ugliness is of form, colour, mode, substance, sensation and utility also. Beauty is never mere appearance. The good is beautiful, and the bad is ugly.

We love what is beautiful in everything and everyone and hate what is ugly in everything and everyone.

The experience of love is a psychological and biological satisfaction but can be found only in and through others and ourselves and is properly a social need.

Our own estimate of our own worth and worthiness is tied up intrinsically with our subjective perception of our individual beauty and ugliness and our own and others' consequent love and hatred for us. It is also tied up in our subjective perception of beauty and ugliness in others and our capacity for love and hatred of others.

Virtue is beautiful and vice ugly. We therefore love virtue and hate vice except where we become envious or jealous of the virtue of others. Jealousy and envy of virtue lead to perversion and self-destruction.

> The good is beautiful.
> All evil is ugly.

Consequently, all sane and rational individuals love good and hate evil.

Joy and pleasure are generally and ultimately good and wholesome and signal the satisfaction of innate human needs, psychological, social or biological.

Joy is psychological pleasure, distinct from sensory or physical pleasure.

The satisfaction of biological needs, such as those for food, drink and sexual union and orgasm lead to corresponding pleasure. Sexual pleasure is also tied to affection and love, in which aspect it is a psychological pleasure or joy.

Happiness, the satisfaction of natural needs and desires, is joy and pleasure and is generally and ultimately good and wholesome.

Unhappiness, the frustration or perversion of natural needs and desires, is pain and suffering and generally and ultimately evil.

Joy and pleasure are generally and ultimately good, as pain and suffering are generally and ultimately evil.

Love longing and loneliness are synonymous. The end of love longing is the end of loneliness. Love longing dies in the gratification of our need to love and be loved and through sexual union with a loved one. Love longing is underlaid by the longing for union with the opposite sex inherent in most of us, which longing is psychological, emotional and sexual.

Convergent with this longing for union with the opposite sex is the longing for psychic union with "God" or Nature and good society.

Psychic union with "God," Spirit and Soul of the Universe, effaces the sexual aspect of love longing and is a great joy.

Love longing and loneliness can die through psychic union with "God" or Nature or friendship in good society.

Parenthood and love of one's children is a very special satisfaction of one's need to love and be loved and of love longing.

Love may be spiritual or sexual.

Spiritual love for the opposite sex becomes sexual love. It acquires aspects of desire and affection, lust and tenderness.

Sexual love leads ultimately through its satisfaction; to spiritual love of the opposite sex.

The frustration or perversion of spiritual or sexual love leads to hatred and alienation from the opposite sex.

We can experience spiritual love of our own sex.

Sexual love of one's own sex is relatively rare yet of some considerable significance for many.

Homosexual love, like heterosexual love, can be both spiritual and sexual.

BIOLOGICAL NEEDS

Biological needs constitute the base of human needs but integrate vertically with psychological and social needs.

Biological needs require certain material preconditions in order to be fulfilled.

Food, clothing, housing and physical security, which are all preconditions of social security, are necessary for the possibility of species reproduction of human beings.

Economic production and distribution underlie the possibility of biological reproduction.

Biological need is inseparable from social and psychological need, and all three aspects are interactive.

If any aspect of need becomes frustrated, then all aspects of need satisfaction are affected.

A person whose need for love or sex is frustrated will not be happy or capable of performing or functioning as a full human being.

A person whose need for psychological orientation in life has been frustrated or perverted will not function as a full human being, either.

Biological need is primarily the need for sexual fulfilment.

BIOLOGICAL NEED HAS TWO ASPECTS TO FULFILMENT

Firstly, the need for frequent sexual copulation and orgasm if neurosis is to be avoided.

Secondly, parenthood. Marriage fulfils both these needs, and as a consequence, is the most enduring of all human relationships.

Marriage cannot be seen, however, merely as the locus of biological fulfilment. It must be seen also as the focus of satisfaction of psychological and social needs of both partners, if it is to endure.

The satisfaction of biological need engenders population and society and is underwritten by economic activity in the face of Nature as a precondition.

Different levels of economic and technological transcendence over Nature by Humanity support different material levels of human subsistence and different scales of biological reproduction.

Birth control distinguishes Humanity from other animal species. It is voluntary and deliberate or necessary control of biological reproduction of humans by humans that most distinguishes Humanity as transcendent.

Other distinguishing features of Humanity are its material productive activity, its capacity to enhance its physical limitations through the making of tools and weapons or of its mental limitations through invention of computers and scientific instruments and also its social organisation in confrontation with other species in the face of Nature.

The Earth is finite and limits the ultimate scale of biological reproduction, except for the possibility of conquest of the Solar System and the Cosmos by human exploration.

Birth control is an urgent imperative for Humanity despite escalating economic productive capacity.

An unfortunate distinguishing feature of Humanity is its capacity and will to kill and exploit Humanity, and that this is not in Humanity's interest is the most potent fact related to peaceful progress, both social and political.

The final distinguishing feature of Humanity is its killing and exploitation of other species in the interest of its own survival.

JUSTICE AND LAW

Justice is such social condition of Humanity as ensures the fulfilment and satisfaction of natural human needs and desires to the extent that vice and crime are non-existent in society.

Justice is such order in society as conditions virtue and humanity among the people.

Justice is such authority as generates peace and harmony in society.

There can be no peace or harmony in society without justice.

Justice rewards virtuous and moral behaviour and punishes or contains vicious or immoral behaviour.

Justice is necessary, since its absence is injustice.

There is no such thing as merely relative justice; justice contains the absolute or is non-existent.

There is that which is just or unjust or that which is neither just nor unjust but neutral.

Justice is the embodiment of the spirit (ethics) in the letter (practice) of the Law.

Justice must not (will not) only be done; it must be (will be) seen to be done.

Justice is relative to the society in which it operates yet contains an element relevant to all historically existent society. It is both absolute and relative, contemporary and eternal.

The implementation of justice is often an evil in itself, e.g. imprisonment or death.

Justice is evil unto evil, which is good.

The worst injustice is such injustice as appears just.

The origin and root of all injustice is the oppression, persecution and exploitation of humans by humans.

Any action committed in the interest of a just cause must be just itself.

Evil unto them who evil intend or commit.

Only the person of evil intentions and actions fears justice.

It is just that the merciful receive clemency and that the unmerciful receive no clemency.

Murder is the killing of the innocent.

Crime ultimately destroys the criminal.

Two wrongs do not make a right; only true justice avenges wrong.

Evil engenders counter evil as its own ultimate destruction.

Good generates good as its own support and ultimate triumph.

The inalienable right of self-defence requires a capacity for evil unto evil.

Good cannot overcome evil; only evil can vanquish evil.

One must develop the capacity for evil unto evil in order to survive.

To do evil unto evil is to do good.

They who live by violence generally die violently.

They who pursue evil pursue it unto their own destruction and death.

Let evil find its own, that the good be spared.

Both evil and good are ultimately material.

Both evil and good are realities and concepts specific and subject to the interest of given classes.

Justice is evil unto evil and promotes good.

Ultimately, Law originates in the need to order social behaviour in the interest of creating and maintaining humane and civilised society, devoid of vice and crime.

Ultimately Law finds its rationale in "moral realism" or humanist ethics.

The Law is above religion, nor can the ethics on which it rests be drawn from any one religion or several.

Law is social necessity of and for civilised and good society.

Law is impotent in the face of war and revolution.

The science of jurisprudence has two aspects - the rational and empirical.

The integration of reason and experience is essential to good Law.

The Law must adhere to the ideal of true Justice as its raison d'etre.

Just legality is essential to peace and harmony and good society.

Law that cannot be implemented with consistency in practice is either farce or oppression and is bad Law.

Bad Law is unjust and immoral and must be opposed until it is changed.

In defending your rights, I defend my own and vice versa.

They only have rights whose rights are defended.

Just legality bestows freedom of moral action and activity on everyone.

The fact that evil engenders evil in opposition to itself, whereas good engenders good in its own support ensures the victory of good over evil in life.